Prophetic Reflections

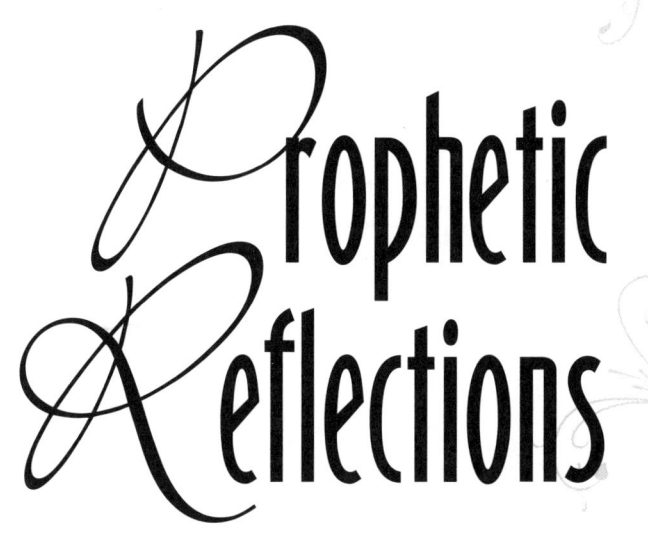

POETRY FROM THE HEART
OF THE PROPHETESS

Debra A. JORDAN

FOGHORN
PUBLISHERS
"Of Making Many Books There Is No End..."

Prophetic Reflections

©2007 by Debra A. Jordan. All Rights Reserved

All Scripture quotations, unless otherwise indicated, are taken from the Holy Bible, New International Version®, NIV® Copyright 1973, 1978, 1984 by International Bible Society; the King James Version, and the Amplified Version. Used by permission.

Prophetic Reflections: Poetry From the Heart of the Prophetess

ISBN-13: 978-1-934466-00-1
ISBN-10: 1-934466-00-X

Zoe Ministries
310 Riverside Drive
New York, NY 10025
(212) 316-2177
(212) 316-5769 (fax)
www.prophetessdebrajordan.com

Foghorn Publishers
P.O. Box 8286
Manchester, CT 06040-0286
860-216-5622
860-568-4821 FAX
foghornpublisher@aol.com

No part of this book may be reproduced or transmitted in any form or by any means, electronic or mechanical, including photocopying, recording, or by any information storage and retrieval system, without permission in writing from the publisher.

1 2 3 4 5 6 7 8 9 10 / 09 08 07

POETRY FROM THE HEART OF THE PROPHETESS

Debra A. JORDAN

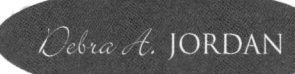

Dedication

I would like to dedicate this book to the two mothers in my life, Mary L. Berrian and Mary L. Jordan. Both of these women are absolutely extraordinary women, whom are constantly an inspiration in my life. Also to my wonderful family, and all of my spiritual mentors who have helped me, and shown me a more excellent way.

Prophetic Reflections

POETRY FROM THE HEART OF THE PROPHETESS

Debra A. JORDAN

Contributors

This is a list of the generous partners that helped to make this book possible.

1. Linda Williams
2. Carolyn Jackson
3. Justine Simmons
4. Gloria Kelley
5. Florence Smith
6. Janice Winbush
7. Tiwana Porter
8. Gladys Austin
9. Mascareen Cohen
10. Debra Campany
11. Aaron Lorna
12. Willie Mae Parris
13. Evelyn L'Elie

Debra A. JORDAN

Contents

Introduction ix
How to Use This Book xiii
Debra's Heaven Garden 1
Pain 5
Time – The Watcher 9
Now Is 13
The Lie 17
Love Song 19
I Thirst 23
Dancing in the Womb of Depression 25
Trees 29
Clutter 31
Life 33
Silence 35
Perfection 37
Evaporation 39
Determination 41
Idols Speaking 43
Be Angry But Sin Not 47
The Law of Protest 51
Woman, Love Thyself (by Joselyn Rodriguez) .53
The Call 57
Mother 61
Let Go 65
I Am 69
Lost 71

Prophetic Reflections

What is Death?	75
Memories	79
Thinking Thoughts	81
Wantings	85
Love is in the Air	89
The Thirst for Life	93
Perplexities	95
Why Are You Committing Crimes Against Yourself?	97
The Drums of Exaltation	101
Marriage	103
The All-Ness	105
Sister Wisdom	107
Rejection	111
A Prayer	113
Essence	117
Innocence	119
Frustration	121
Age	125
Who?	127
Love Walk	131
My Confession	133
Illuminations	137
The Viewer	141
Who Do Men Say I Am?	145
Unstoppable and Invinciple	149
Me	151
Talking Rivers	155
My Soul	159

POETRY FROM THE HEART OF THE PROPHETESS

Debra A. JORDAN

Introduction

Poetry is one of the oldest art forms utilizing language to communicate an ostensible and sometimes hidden meaning. Some believe that poetry may even be older than literacy. Within literate cultures poetry appears in some of the earliest records. The meaning in poetry is very unique in that the message being conveyed can be provocative, folksy, or even prophetically revelatory. When poetry reveals a hidden truth, most commonly that truth is usually about oneself and ones awareness about themselves and the world around them. To that end poetry can be used as a tool to help better our society, if only we hear its message and take heed.

In the bible there are four basic kinds of poetry, speculative, lyrical, folklore, and prophetical. In *Prophetic Reflections: Poetry From the Heart of The Prophetess,* I speak in poetry the sentiments of my deepest heart, messages that communicate some of the most challenging subjects that life confronts us with.

Prophetic Reflections

In every poem I introduce the problem and within the same meter offer the age-old solution—to look within yourself and discover. Unlike other kinds of poetry, prophetic poetry is expressed only through the eyes of the seer. A seer is one who hears from God and is then mandated to take the message to the world.

Jeremiah the prophet is one such example of one whose works and prophecies are thoroughly poetical and full of prose. A major portion of the Old Testament was written in a poetical format especially with regards to the books that heralded the message of Messiah coming forth. Even in our modern era, there are still many poets that are seers, speaking forth a message of liberation, forgiveness, hope, and transformation. A few of these poetic seers are Maya Angelou, Alice Walker, Nikki Giovanni, Phyllis Wheatley, Langston Hughes, Homer, and even William Shakespeare. One cannot deny the preponderance that each of these writers has had on society, even in shaping the way we think.

POETRY FROM THE HEART OF THE PROPHETESS

Debra A. JORDAN

How To Use This Book

Since nothing happens in life without a thought first preceding it, I have created a book of poetry designed to do exactly that. I have included 52 of my most beloved works in this volume. I've chosen 52 poems to coincide with the weeks in a year. That's right, you have an entire year to complete this book. Since repetition is the mother of skill and the brooding ground of all human character, you are going to master each poem by repeating it each day for a week. You'll have weekends off to relax and meditate on what your new thought is for the week. Monday through Friday, you need to read the same poem. Each day, you will have a different thought or perspective about what you have read.

Whatever, thought comes to mind; you must write it down in your journal directly next to the day. You

Prophetic Reflections

need not write an essay, but rather your simple concise thoughts. The thoughts that you have will actually make this book a collective effort between you and me, helping to rewrite your life through the power of prophetic poetry. You may ask, "What if I do not have any thoughts on a particular day?" Great question! Don't force it.

If an idea or concept comes to you, then write it down. If not, then that is fine also. The whole process is about developing you, and that may happen in very different ways depending on the person and their personal experience. Remember, these are my intuitive reflections. Yours may vary. My hope for you is that through your reading of this collection of poems that you will discover a totally new you in the process.

Prophetess Debra A. Jordan
Saddle River, New Jersey

Debra's Heaven Garden

*A*ll the gates are open, for I stand at the gate to welcome all who desire to come in; for no one will be denied. For in Debra's heaven, everything that is needed readily appears. For I give freely and lay no charge or offense to anyone. There is only one price exacted; the willingness to partake of life. For I say to one and all, "Come! For the Spirit does beckon thee!" It's a call to spirit, for Spirit only speaks to spirit.

Are you weary? Tired of living in despair and hopelessness? I say and command you to lift your eyes and see your salvation, for it is present and available.

Allow me to embrace you and impart strength and newness to you, for I am Spirit, and I am Love. Hear my wisdom and defer not from it. Come and rest and refresh yourself, for this is an easy thing that I ask of you.

Prophetic Reflections

Come cry your tears, and weep for what's inside of you, for the tears will bring forth joy, and the weeping will change you through and through. Don't be afraid to lie down and rest, for the rest is needed to bring the release.

I say to the daughters of righteousness, "Stand strong in your anointing;" and to the daughters of Sarah, "Keep thy charge, for obedience is the honorable way of transformation."

I say to my elders and to my younglings, "We are one. We have been given a great command and that is to help and teach each other. There is neither time nor space in my heaven garden, for there shall be honor and glory from generation to generation, with joy unspeakable forever more."

Peace

Debra A. JORDAN

Weekly Journal

Monday
_____
_____
_____

Tuesday
_____
_____
_____

Wednesday
_____
_____
_____

Thursday
_____
_____
_____

Friday
_____
_____
_____

Debra's Heaven Garden

Prophetic Reflections

POETRY FROM THE HEART OF THE PROPHETESS

Pain

Pain comes from the non-acceptance of its voice. The pain of the body, both physical and emotional, wants to survive; the desire and the needs are all fighting for survival and want to be heard. Illusions of falsehood from you only initiate destructive attitudes, ideas and thoughts. Come away, My Beloved! Abandon the distortions of anger, jealousy, pain, and negativity, for they feed upon the banquet of pain.

No one is conscious of your pain; you must bring your pain body into the light in order to deal with it. The pains of the bodies become both the perpetrator and the victim....

All pain is ultimately a deception, but you must first come to a place of recognition and sit upon the threshold of confrontation. You must observe it and then deal with it in the present. Have you become the

Prophetic Reflections

watcher? Watching signifies acceptance. Have you lost your move?

The pain body is expressed by the unconscious and revealed by the conscious. You must become the guardian of your inner consciousness.

How does fear arrive? Isn't it healthy?

You can always cope with the now, but not the future.

Fear is the ultimate state of the ego fearing Death. The ego seeks to live, thereby lifting itself and living for itself by any means necessary.

Power over others is fear disguising itself as strength.

As long as the ego and mind are ruling your life, you will not find true happiness. There will always be the pain of loneliness and emptiness. The ego attaches itself to the larger illusionary self. See yourself within the joys of life and then lose yourself within them.

Debra A. JORDAN

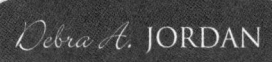

Weekly Journal

Monday

_____
_____
_____

Tuesday

_____
_____
_____

Wednesday

_____
_____
_____

Thursday

_____
_____
_____

Friday

_____
_____
_____

Pain

Prophetic Reflections

POETRY FROM THE HEART OF THE PROPHETESS

Debra A. Jordan

Time-The Watcher

Time and mind are inseparable. The past gives you identification and the future gives you a chance to wish and to hope. Time is the illusion. Timelessness hides in forms, lest they do appear.

This present moment is all the time you will ever have. Time is the cause of your suffering and problems; time is still and will always be attached to the past and future. There is no salvation in time - you can only receive your salvation in the now.

Physiological time is the past and the future all wrapped up into one. Hope keeps your focus on the future...

Prophetic Reflections

Your life situations are full of problems; there are no answers for the solutions, for they are stuck in time, whereas your life is the now.

The present and the now are one and the same. You'll arrive in the present by just being in the now. You must have your existence in the now. You must say YES to the moments....

It is as it is. You must allow your present existence to be. You must accept the present as it is; make it your friend and not your enemy. You must be able to access the present of the now...

You must allow things to be and be within in order to experience the Now. You must awaken out of the sphere of time and walk into the now. You must realize that problems do not exist- there is just the now of being-ness. Problems are man-made and must be dealt with in the now-ness. The mind loves problems; it gives the mind a sense of being and aliveness.

> *Thought: Time robs you from the present now-ness. Time keeps you from meeting deadlines and keeps you looking. It refuses to give you the ability to just be.*

Debra A. JORDAN

Weekly Journal

Monday

Tuesday

Wednesday

Thursday

Friday

Time-The Watcher

Prophetic Reflections

12

POETRY FROM THE HEART OF THE PROPHETESS

Now Is

The key to the spiritual dimension is the NOW.

Suffering needs to live in the past; it cannot live in the now. "If not now, then when?"

Past and future burns in the essence of time.

Meister Eckhart said "Time is the essence that keeps us from God."

Timeless dimension is a realm of all that is.

Step out the dimension of the past and future.

Past and present are illusions.

Be present for the watcher of the mind.

Become aware of what you are feeling and observing.

Clock time includes learning from your past and taking appropriate actions. Setting goals is clock time, and yet they still honor the now.

Prophetic Reflections

The future is a replica of the past.

You must be willing to access the now in order to change the past and create your future.

The only place where the past can be changed is hidden within your degree of apprehending the consciousness of the now.

Debra A. JORDAN

Weekly Journal

Monday

Tuesday

Wednesday

15

Thursday

Friday

Now Is

Debra A. JORDAN

The Lie

So... you are trying to befriend me. You are always knocking on my door, desiring to come into my garden of Imagination. You say you love me, you say you care about me; you even say that you can help me. You have even tried to enter my domain uninvited.

So you come to me this day dressed in beauty and light. Your apparel was and is altogether perfect. For with my eyes I see no flaw; you are boundless and enclosed in expectation and secrecy. You have dressed itself up, to be called by another name, other than its own name....

It has tried to call it the names that I so dearly love and uphold...

Prophetic Reflections

Weekly Journal

Monday

_____
_____
_____

Tuesday

_____
_____
_____

Wednesday

_____
_____
_____

Thursday

_____
_____
_____

Friday

_____
_____
_____

POETRY FROM THE HEART OF THE PROPHETESS

Debra A. JORDAN

Love Song

I remember the time when we two stood on the banks of the river called Euphrates. It was a time of war and a time of peace. Everyone walked and understood in the way they thought was right and just. The sun and moon did shine upon thy strength and thy might. Oh, what majesty it was in all its glory! I beheld thy strength and began to melt inside. I cried and wept, longing for your embrace. For your countenance did speak a language of reassurance. Your spirit did stand above the heights, and your soul did speak love to my soul. For there was a holy joining and marriage between our souls that would last throughout eternity.

We need not speak in words, for our spirits already knew what we both knew eons ago; we were meant to be together in whatever form we chose to appear.

Ah! I remember that day very well as you approached, my tall, dark and full of light hero. The force of thy

Prophetic Reflections

presence brought pure joy to my innermost being. I relish the fact that I was the one chosen and appointed for this great union. I was elated, knowing that nothing and no one could stop this destiny. It was you and I, I and you, standing toe to toe; looking at each other eye to eye. We both knew that we had to fulfill the call.

Ah! The Divine endowed us with the privilege of tasting and exploring each other through and through! You touched me, and the hot pain-pleasure of ecstasy overflowed my being. Our lips touched, and exploded with the fire of timeless passion.

We made love all night; that starry night. We sipped the wine of love into the morning as we discovered each other from top to bottom and bottom to top.

Let us lie in the field all day and all night — let us become drunk in each other's embrace. Let us become enamored with the moment. Let us command the sun and the moon to stand still, for time should cease as we make sweet love until we want no more. Yea, though time arouses from its slumber, our love will last throughout eternity.

Debra A. JORDAN

Weekly Journal

Monday

_____
_____
_____

Tuesday

_____
_____
_____

Wednesday

_____
_____
_____

Thursday

_____
_____
_____

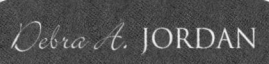

Friday

_____
_____
_____

Love Song

Debra A. JORDAN

I Thirst

I was dry and thirsty and eager to partake. You, my beloved, came and quenched my thirst, for I am full from your touch. Your smell lingers throughout my day. My imagination is already complete in you. Please touch me and hold me, my Love. Let us .....

Prophetic Reflections

Weekly Journal

Monday

_____
_____
_____

Tuesday

_____
_____
_____

Wednesday

_____
_____
_____

Thursday

_____
_____
_____

Friday

_____
_____
_____

POETRY FROM THE HEART OF THE PROPHETESS

Debra A. JORDAN

Dancing in the Womb of Depression

I am merely breathing and surviving. Will I ever LIVE in the midst of these things? I don't know where or how. Which way do I go? My heart desires to turn and run from this dilemma? I need to breathe. I need to speak. I MUST BE HEARD. Why? I don't know.

I am at peace with God and with man, yet a war is still raging. Am I at peace with myself? Am I at war with a lie I cannot identify?

I know with a surety that my peace, God's peace, shall not leave me nor will it forsake me....

My love is complete and whole, for it is pure through and through. I will not be afraid, nor dismayed, but I

Prophetic Reflections

shall stand upon my ground. I shall wait until my change comes, for it's already here. The arms of transformation have already possessed me and embraced me.

Have I lost myself? Have I become so involved and blind to materiality that I don't know or understand where I start or where I end? I dare not say I'm confused, for I am not. Nor am I faint-hearted. I don't know. I feel overwhelmed and yet I feel the Spirit of Liberty and Grace pushing forward within me. Spirit will not allow me to stay down, for I must rise up and praise My God, for I know in whom I believe. I shall stretch out, move forward, reach up, and DANCE!!

Weekly Journal

Monday

_____
_____
_____

Tuesday

_____
_____
_____

Wednesday

_____
_____
_____

Thursday

_____
_____
_____

Friday

_____
_____
_____

Debra A. JORDAN

Trees

Trees, trees! Hide me! Trees, trees! Cover me! Trees! Speak to me! Trees, oh trees! Fall upon me - don't be afraid. You stand strong in majesty and in beauty. I am not afraid, for I have watched and observed you. Teach me your strength, for I long to stand tall as you, even in my weakest state. I long to stand upon my pillars, to do what I must....

Prophetic Reflections

Weekly Journal

Monday

_____
_____
_____

Tuesday

_____
_____
_____

Wednesday

_____
_____
_____

Thursday

_____
_____
_____

Friday

_____
_____
_____

POETRY FROM THE HEART OF THE PROPHETESS

Debra A. JORDAN

Clutter

Clutter... so much clutter... here, there, and everywhere. Looking here, far and near, my eyes see only the mess.

I said to the stranger, "Please help me to clean this stuff."

He looked at me with gentle eyes and a wistful smile and said,

"The clutter and the mess you think you see,

It's there because you wanted it to be.

Once you say within yourself, 'Be gone and do not return;'

"It will vaporize right before your glistening eyes."

Prophetic Reflections

Weekly Journal

Monday

_____
_____
_____

Tuesday

_____
_____
_____

Wednesday

_____
_____
_____

Thursday

_____
_____
_____

Friday

_____
_____
_____

POETRY FROM THE HEART OF THE PROPHETESS

Life

LIFE. Life. Life, speak to me and allow me to hear your voice.
Life should be lived, not loved.

Life is sweet as it gives forth its nectar. We are to drink of life essences.

For as life unfold her petals, many just look and say "How nice and how beautiful."

They inhale life fragrances and linger, knowing not that they are to partake and make room for others to come.

Life is a giver not a taker.

Her arms are stretched out to receive all who would say "yes" unto her.

My heart and mind are open to take possession of all her manifold wisdom.

Help me to know.

Even as *I Am* known.

Prophetic Reflections

Weekly Journal

Monday

_____
_____
_____

Tuesday

_____
_____
_____

Wednesday

_____
_____
_____

Thursday

_____
_____
_____

Friday

_____
_____
_____

POETRY FROM THE HEART OF THE PROPHETESS

Silence

Silence is man's quest for selflessness. It is not something that can be obtained in a day or night, but it is the quest of a life long journey. Man's aim isn't to search for silence, but to become it. To be swallowed and totally encompassed with the bliss and beauty of utter stillness. Then, and only then, will man open the door to ecstasy. Blissfulness is sweet and contagious. To harmonize within this realm of nothingness and yet all-ness is to cease from trivial decay.

Cease from struggles and toiling, and let there be …. Change will come in its fullness. Silence just is. It doesn't try to be, it just simply is. Silence is not a person or thing, but it is unutterable happiness.

Prophetic Reflections

Weekly Journal

Monday

Tuesday

Wednesday

Thursday

Friday

POETRY FROM THE HEART OF THE PROPHETESS

Debra A. JORDAN

Perfection

To be or not to be, that is the question to the answer....
To become is to die — to become void, and empty inside — to dwell in the loneliness.

To experience the powerless of the nothingness.

To have power is to not be in control.

To long for death is to seek after life....for life is death.

What we seek to save we shall surely lose, and what we seek to lose, we shall also find. Change is always appearing and disappearing, for it is the manifold wisdom of the Infinite One. We experience change in different realms and ways.

Awareness brings forth conclusions....

My reality is…

Change does not dwell within a place or person; it just is.

Prophetic Reflections

Weekly Journal

Monday

_____
_____
_____

Tuesday

_____
_____
_____

Wednesday

_____
_____
_____

Thursday

_____
_____
_____

Friday

_____
_____
_____

POETRY FROM THE HEART OF THE PROPHETESS

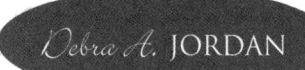

Evaporation

Today I can truly rejoice, for I know in Whom I believe. I heard a man of God speak wonderfully today. I was truly blessed. For some reason, he started out talking about relationship, and then moved into the remainder of his message.

I am free; the tears of sadness have evaporated in the heat of peace. Things and situations no longer matter, and yet I know that they do. I know who I am by the grace of God. No more trying to figure out what I did wrong or right. Life is about growth, and I know that I'm growing and evolving into my Christhood by my Savior's undying love for me.

Prophetic Reflections

Weekly Journal

Monday

_____
_____
_____

Tuesday

_____
_____
_____

Wednesday

_____
_____
_____

Thursday

_____
_____
_____

Friday

_____
_____
_____

POETRY FROM THE HEART OF THE PROPHETESS

Debra A. JORDAN

Determination

Rejoice! I say, and again I say, rejoice! "For it's not by might, nor by power, but by My Spirit," saith the Lord of Hosts. It seems that I am always writing when things are in turmoil, or when distress disturbs my relationships. There are so many things that I don't understand and yet I am compelled to make decisions. Why? I don't seem to know or understand.

I am determined that I shall praise the Name of the Lord. For I am nothing, nor do I have anything without Him. I am an empty shell. I await to be filled, for the Infinite One is the Only One. For I shall stand in the congregation of the Almighty, and declare His Word and works forever....

Prophetic Reflections

Weekly Journal

Monday

_____
_____
_____

Tuesday

_____
_____
_____

Wednesday

_____
_____
_____

Thursday

_____
_____
_____

Friday

_____
_____
_____

POETRY FROM THE HEART OF THE PROPHETESS

Debra A. JORDAN

"Idols Speaking"

What Happens When Your Idol Speaks?

Don't allow the illusions and the idleness of your imagination to become your realities. It's the falsehood of your truth. It is what will keep you trapped in the vise of want and desire.

God will give you the desires of your heart. But in wanting, we must make sure that the desire has been birthed by the Father, and not by your flesh. The Scripture says there is no good thing in the flesh. There are many things, issues, hopes, dreams, desires, wishes and aspirations that we all have. Many of these lie dormant, or rest in the cavernous recesses of our subconscious mind.

At every stage and level you will always be tested to see if your dream, hope, desire, wish, or aspiration is an "Ishmael" or an "Isaac." "Ishmael" was produced after the order of the flesh. "Isaac" was produced after the

Prophetic Reflections

order of the Spirit. Spirit always has a way of coming forth out of that which seems dead and inactive. The "Ishmael" can never walk in the promise. God said, "Isaac have *I* loved, but Ishmael have I hated."

Debra A. JORDAN

Weekly Journal

Monday

Tuesday

Wednesday

Thursday

Friday

"Idols Speaking"

Debra A. JORDAN

"Be Angry But Sin Not…"

Discourse: To Myself, With Myself

You said that you were "angry." Does that make it right to utter jagged words and accusations? Words have life. God has given man the power of speech. Man has the ability to speak and to imagine whatsoever he pleases. Man has the creative capacity to create with his mouth.

Anger causes you to speak, act and to erupt with the truth of the unexpressed that hides inside of you. It draws out the truth you really feel and think. Anger doesn't tell you whether you are right or wrong, but it hastens that which you have been avoiding; that which you have been unable and unwilling to deal with under normal conditions. Anger says either you deal with me now or I will deal with you later….

Prophetic Reflections

Anger comes to show you what's lurking within your temple. Anger comes to reveal what's been growing and harboring inside of you. Anger is that delicate surgical tool which is used to stir up the rotting sediments that collect at the bottom of the glass. Once the sediment has been stirred up, the liquid becomes murky and cloudy. Once the mirror has been marred, no one can see in view a definable image.

Anger is an indicator. It shows issues that need to be dealt with. The main concern here is "trust." Trust is the glue that keeps relationships together.

Anger is the catalyst for change and reconciliation. Anger cries to be whole again. Anger causes you to eliminate garbage out of your system. Anger is the instrument used to purge the emotions. Anger is a healthy emotion that forces all unsettled issues out of your bodies.

Be angry, but sin not. Anger is a natural phenomenon, for it's an aspect of God. Even if it brings death, as God did with the flood, God was awesome enough to repent. Therefore I say it's ok to be angry and to make a mistake, but not to the point of sinning, but after the act.

In the sex act, there are different phases, but the best phase is the after play, for it solidifies the total act. It becomes the "amen" and the "so be it." The after play reconciles the two into oneness, it's the "Ah" of God. The "Ah" is the flowing in and out. It brings preservation to the union.

Debra A. JORDAN

Be angry, but sin not. It's not your place to call forth vengeance. God will do that. Anger causes you to forget the divine Self. Anger reduces you to bestiality. Anger can be uncontrollable and it can consume you and others. I believe that right belongs to only to God.

Anger yes, but sin will destroy and dissolve that which is precious to you and to everyone else that's around you. The sin is the accusation. You said, "I was angry." That's well and good, but to respond as someone who doesn't know the way, or to further lay charge to someone, as to judge them from your emotions and not from your divinity, that is sin unto you. To judge someone from your humanity and not from your divinity is truly unrighteous. To function in anger is like functioning as a slanderer. A slanderer kills three individuals with one deadly stroke. Words have the power to pull down, and destroy the very being of the individual. The bible says that life and death is in the power of the tongue. Words have the potential not just to fracture your bones, but they can rupture and devastate your spirit also. You don't have to be physical — your words will cause great damage and harm to you. When we speak, we should always bring forth life.

Prophetic Reflections

Weekly Journal

Monday

_____
_____
_____

Tuesday

_____
_____
_____

Wednesday

_____
_____
_____

Thursday

_____
_____
_____

Friday

_____
_____
_____

POETRY FROM THE HEART OF THE PROPHETESS

Debra A. JORDAN

The Law of Protest

There's the question of trust. Why do I allow anyone to make me feel small and low. I keep feeling that when any and everything happens, you see me as the one to blame. It's seems that I'm the one at fault. I don't know if you are trying to show me or teach me the "do's" and "don'ts." I will proclaim it and shout it on the mountain top that you are truly my teacher and instructor. You have taught me through your actions and through your deeds. I have also learned from you in your accomplishment that you should never allow anyone to make you feel lower or insignificant, or to make you feel that you have no rights. You taught me never to allow people to insinuate something concerning me; not to sit back and do nothing.

Does the Law of Protest ever apply to me?

Prophetic Reflections

Weekly Journal

Monday

Tuesday

Wednesday

Thursday

Friday

POETRY FROM THE HEART OF THE PROPHETESS

Debra A. JORDAN

Woman, Love Thyself

I awaken unto my Self
And receive the part of me that I have not known...
For so many years,
Through the shedding of wasted tears,
I thought my Emotions were full grown.

I broke the mirror of perception, many years ago
Because of the image I chose not to know....
My subconscious image
Never met my conscious goal..
I hated the Me that I had to face,
Way down deep from my mind, my body, and my soul.

I could never see the perfection
So I embraced self-hatred and rejection
My gatekeepers became my worst enemies
Because of their piercing points of view....

Prophetic Reflections

Until one day, a Mirror Image came before me.
It was an Image reflection I could not break;
It showed me the Self I chose to ignore
And the image called "MY NAME" perfect
For my sake.....

It was unfamiliar, yet familiar to me
For what the image showed me was myself;
The true beauty that was never quite evident to me
A light came through and shone upon my face:
And in an instant, I finally understood My place....
My purpose, My reason, and the necessity of my being
This all came about when I took the veil of rejection
and despair off
And I started seeing my True Self...

I came to my Self, and there was not a flaw to be found
I realized the importance of my body
And all it's virtue;
The tears began to fall,
When I realized....
NO!! I am not ugly at all!

This time my tears were not wasted,
I released the pain my body had tasted..
My God,!! My God!! I have searched but could not find,
The greatness of who You have created in me
But now I realize and know I was Blind...

Behold a new creature is formed!
Because the womb of my acceptance
No longer mourns...

POETRY FROM THE HEART OF THE PROPHETESS

Debra A. JORDAN

I am healed!
Fearfully and wonderfully!
And the price?
My body has been redeemed
I now love myself—
Forever whole and complete;
Because now, I see.....

By Jocelyn Rodriquez ©1998

SZURDEE~ {Joselyn Rodriguez} "Living Scribe Productions"1999

Prophetic Reflections

Weekly Journal

Monday

_____
_____
_____

Tuesday

_____
_____
_____

Wednesday

_____
_____
_____

Thursday

_____
_____
_____

Friday

_____
_____
_____

POETRY FROM THE HEART OF THE PROPHETESS

Debra A. JORDAN

The Call

"Listen to My Voice and hear Me well, for there is a call to join in the ranks of the One that has uttered. It is the ones who have not failed in their task, for you are victorious.

Life does not play favorites. Life is a flow of the essence of Spirit. Life places a kiss on the lips of every soul. There is an inner strength that you must embrace, for as you reach toward it, the arms of Strength shall tightly embrace you and will not let you go.

Hear me now, for you stand not alone. Open up your eyes and see…

The wind does blow; the storm does bellow with great intensity and strength.

Everything around me is changing and moving — nothing is ever the same. Life evolves within each blinking movement of the moment.

Prophetic Reflections

But what does this mean? Am I to sit become nothing more than the watcher and the spectator? I am in the midst of the rituals of life......

Debra A. JORDAN

Weekly Journal

Monday

_____
_____
_____

Tuesday

_____
_____
_____

Wednesday

_____
_____
_____

Thursday

_____
_____
_____

Friday

_____
_____
_____

The Call

Prophetic Reflections

60

POETRY FROM THE HEART OF THE PROPHETESS

Debra A. JORDAN

Mother

Shsh! Shsh! For she calls me – yes, she beckons me to come. Shsh! For she has need of me; she beckons me to quiet myself. Oh I know she sees and she is acquainted with my pain. For she looks and walks just like me – is this me or is it another? How can this be?

Stop! Don't you dare run away from her! Don't you dare ignore her call! She cares for us all. Oh, I know who she is! It's Mother! It's Me in another form! It's my form of experience wanting to bring forth the explanation.

Mother cares about our pain. She seeks only to soothe away the memories of the past and to make it right. She's here to cheer you up and to send you on your merry journey.

Stop tiptoeing in her Presence. Stop trying to hide yourself from her eyes of wisdom. She will not hurt you; she wants to heal you and to make you whole again.

Prophetic Reflections

You don't have to doubt her abilities, for She can be trusted. Believe in her skills and abilities, for She knows all things. Allow the mask to be removed, and allow the veil of transparency to be lifted. For Mother knows and sees all things past, present, and future. She is truly The Every Seeing Eye. She comes to instruct you in the way of your destiny and purpose

Debra A. JORDAN

Weekly Journal

Monday

Tuesday

Wednesday

Thursday

Friday

Mother

Debra A. JORDAN

Let Go

Why are you screaming and fighting with your destiny? You can't run from yourself. There are many strange, yet familiar voices that are calling me to let go.

Hmph! Why should I let go, when holding on is my stabilizing force of hope? You say it's a false hope, but I say it allows me to smile. What? I know that I am walking in the dark and my frustration is causing me horrific unrest.

"I say again and again, "LET GO" so you can find yourself, LET GO so you can walk into your destiny. The act of Letting Go will allow you to fall into the hands of the infinite, allowing you to open up to new realities and behold new vistas. Stop holding on to false realities, for they are the fairy tales of make believe. Take a leap of faith into the Hand of Divine Care.

God gives you peace and strength to bring about your own liberation. Freedom undulates, (sweet and glorious!), for restrictions and safeguards have vanished. The Voice of Imagination beckons us all.

Debra A. JORDAN

Weekly Journal

Monday

___

Tuesday

___

Wednesday

___

Thursday

___

Friday

___

Let Go

I Am

I Am the Beginning, and yet I Am the Middle and the End. I Am far and yet so very near. I Am all things and yet I Am no-thing in the all-ness of My Very Being. What is My Name? I Am known by many, for it is in the simplicity of My Very Being that I name Myself. I Am The Faceless, for I wear the mask of all those I walk with and who are connected to My Essence. No one can see My Face and understand the complexity of My Very Nature, for it is within the matrix of wonderment that My True Face does appear.

Prophetic Reflections

Weekly Journal

Monday

Tuesday

Wednesday

Thursday

Friday

POETRY FROM THE HEART OF THE PROPHETESS

Debra A. JORDAN

"Lost"

Heart is heavy; where can I go but to the Lord; for He's my all in all. Change isn't easy, but it is necessary. You can either flow with change, or be broken, bruised, shattered and destroyed by its insistence. Change is a very powerful force; it is impersonal. Some say change is good and is very vital to the development of us all.

If change is good, why do I want to run from myself? For myself is God in all its wonder and diverseness. Why do I not want to express my divinity, for that too, is myself in all its expression of beauty?

I feel old. I am in despair. I do not know which way to go. I ask myself why, and yet I do not know. I know, but I am confounded in my own understanding. For those things I esteem have dried up. They have withered; they are wafting to the ground, never to rise again. Oh, where can I or what can I say? Woe is me, for I am undone. I now know that I'm the one in the dark; I am the blind

Prophetic Reflections

one. I'm all-alone; all by myself. I reach out, but there's none to embrace me; none to hold me. I cannot bear to embrace the emptiness of the darkness. I know that in the Light there is warmth, but not for me, for it is, I and I alone that is left standing.

I now know that my heart has betrayed me. Who and what can I now trust in? I'm stuck in a place I know not, for my speech is silence and has become a foreign voice within my own head. Oh, what am I to do? I hear a still small Voice that says, "Stand still and see Me."

Woe is me, for what I believed and thought is gone. My very foundation has been shaken and is no more.

I sit and gaze upon a blank screen — there's nothing there. I revisit my illusion, wanting to hold to my own realities, which are not. Why Father? I can't forget; the piercing words that are a constant reminder to me. This time it's different. Why? I don't know— Have I have been denying the true reality of everything? Or am I choosing to live the lie instead of the truth? Or is it that I have been sleeping and I just woke up? Or is this just a dream from which I cannot awake...I know what I must do. I must shake myself out of the drowsiness and the stupor that I, and I alone have place myself in. Life is calling....

Debra A. JORDAN

Weekly Journal

Monday

___

___

___

Tuesday

___

___

___

Wednesday

___

___

___

Thursday

___

___

___

Friday

___

___

___

"Lest"

Debra A. JORDAN

What is Death?

Death is the stripping away of all that is not you.

The secret is to die before you die.

Death is the fulfillment of the testament of your life.

Death is the decree of divorce that you give to your life experiences.

Death is the final journey that we must take by ourselves and for ourselves.

Death is a void; it is the empty of the essence of life.

Death is your formal awakening from the sleep of separation from Divinity.

Death is the existing door to realities and to the falsehoods that you hold so dear.

Death often masquerades as an enemy and attempts to strike fear and dread within the hearts of men.

Prophetic Reflections

Death taunts us all with the pain of separation, and mocks our attachments to all that is living by infusing dread into the core of our emotions.

Death elicits an answer from us all. I refuse to cower and cringe, for I do not wish to entertain Death. I shall antagonize Death, for I acquainted with Eternal Mystery. Let me go and ascend! I shall take flight and soar into the heavens! I shall open my eyes and behold the truth of life, for it was only just a dream. For I know the Mystery of Dichotomy—- I never left Home, for I have always been eternally alive within my Father's Presence.

Debra A. JORDAN

Weekly Journal

Monday

_____
_____
_____

Tuesday

_____
_____
_____

Wednesday

_____
_____
_____

Thursday

_____
_____
_____

Friday

_____
_____
_____

What is Wealth?

Debra A. JORDAN

Memories

I stand upon the banks of the River of Life, collecting my children who have stayed from my side, and securing those who have gone astray. I will not turn any away, for I call every one of you to come so that I may heal the wounds of your hearts, and restore the fractured images of your personhood. Memories are forever. They don't die and disappear, nor are they transitory moments residing in the shadows of your mind. Your memories are the recording angels of your past selves; I must unchain and free them so that we can become whole and complete once again. I must reconcile them back to the Father. Memories are our deeds, words, actions, and imaginations that have taken on lives of their own. Some of my children choose to stay in the recesses of my past self, but others choose to continue to live in my present state of being-ness; they seem determined to keep me from fulfilling my task at hand. My sweet and bitter memories are just my children voicing their very own opinions which are always waiting for action. They desire to be seen and crave attention, but there must always be the returning back to the Life Source.

Prophetic Reflections

Weekly Journal

Monday

Tuesday

Wednesday

Thursday

Friday

POETRY FROM THE HEART OF THE PROPHETESS

Debra A. JORDAN

Thinking Thoughts

The thoughts of my creative imagination are walking inside of me. It is with my thoughts that I choose to create. It is with my thoughts that I choose to become. It is my thoughts of imagination that are readying themselves, for they desire to be revealed.

I'm thinking, "What if...?" But in creation, the "What if?" always becomes the thoughts of my foundation. I am building and constructing whatever I desire; but it's not made with my two hands. Everything I design and construct is with the skilled and invisible hands of my wonderful imagination. I don't know exactly how the process comes about, if it's my thinking or my thoughts that cause my creation to come into manifestation. I only know that my thinking and my thoughts have entwined themselves. They are no longer separate

Prophetic Reflections

entities but they have become unified in the marriage of all things. Therefore they/it have become my reality; for I am beholding it and touching it and there's no denying it.

Debra A. JORDAN

Weekly Journal

Monday

_____
_____
_____

Tuesday

_____
_____
_____

Wednesday

_____
_____
_____

Thursday

_____
_____
_____

Friday

_____
_____
_____

Thinking Thoughts

Wantings

Hold me...love me... don't ever let me go.....
Say, "Yes," and then I'll know that everything will be alright.

Say, "Yes," for I know that the two of us can withstand an army.

We will endure the fire and the storms of life. My beloved, it's in our conforming ordaining love that we never die, for we were meant to be.

Say, "Yes," for we will make every crooked path straight; for "Yes" is our very soul cry, united and joining itself to Oneness. "Yes" is our Alpha and our Omega. It is within the sweet surrender that we create new realities. Please say "Yes," and mean it with your whole heart, for it is then that we take the wings of an eagle and soar into the heavens of our destiny. "Yes" will cause us to turn into the essentiality of the Light and the Life of God. For we are two beacons of light, awaiting to be converted into the Great Light;

Prophetic Reflections

Say, "Yes," and release the treasures, for they are the sensual pleasures of life.

Say, "Yes," and I will be faithful and true forever more, for I am incomplete without you.

Please say yes, for there's no one else for me. I would be void and empty without you in my life. I will never let you go, for we were meant for each other before the foundation of the earth. Together we will see, hear, and walk in happiness and love. The question was asked, and I will answer the question yet again....Yes, my love....

Say, "Yes," for we discovered a precious treasure; we complete one another. Having found you, my love, is finding and reawakening my soul unto salvation; for when I found you, I discovered myself.

Hold me....love me.... don't ever let me go.....

Debra A. JORDAN

Weekly Journal

Monday

Tuesday

Wednesday

Thursday

Friday

Wantings

Debra A. JORDAN

Love is in the Air

I bathe myself in the beauty of God's creation, and cavort in the uniqueness of my being. I know who and what I am, for of a surety, I make my boast in the one that brings oneness to my spirit, soul and body. There is excitement all around us; we are vibrating on the frequency of love. I love your smile, for it brings light and laughter to my day. The twinkle in your eyes tells me that all is well. I love your strength, because it's always readily available. I love your unfaltering confidence that you have in our God. Your faith and belief in the Omnipotence of God is the Completing Force of who we are. Our love isn't mere words, nor is it embodied in our deeds. Our love is so powerful that it causes the sun to shine through the droplets of rain; our love removes every cloud that dares to cast a shadow. I love your strength that's readily available. Our love is the pure essence of life unfolding. What we feel and know to be true is that retreat is illegal; we push forward in our love for each other. There can't be any selfishness, but only the eager gift and sacrifice of ourselves. Our love is much greater than we can imagine or comprehend. Our love is the fulfilling sustenance of God; for Love is the greatest Force that forever guides us. Love is the fulfilling Life Force of God that never seeks to please Itself, but only to give freely of itself. Love is always willing and able to sacrifice itself. Together, we create new life and purpose. We breathe life into future events. No one can withstand or defeat us, for our love is invincible.

Love causes us to return back to the Father. My darling, what we have is special, and it will only increase with intensity as time goes by.

Debra A. JORDAN

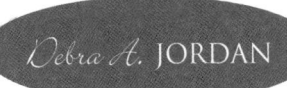

Weekly Journal

Monday

Tuesday

Wednesday

Thursday

Friday

Love is in the Air

Debra A. JORDAN

The Thirst for Life

Nothing is ever so dear than the thirst of life wanting to be quenched. It's a soul that has forgotten from whence it has come and is devoid of purpose. The very thing I behold is what I so desire and long for every moment of my existence. In my reaching, I touch the nothingness that encompasses me. It's of a truth that if I continue on my journey, I shall be filled, but I must stay on my path. I cast off the weights that have sought to keep me down, and I arise upon the newness of the wings of the morning; for no one or nothing can stop me. I say to myself," Get up, for all is not lost." It is the belief that tells me to continue my present journey. It is my faith that says, "The Lord is My Shepherd and I shall not want."

Prophetic Reflections

Weekly Journal

Monday

_____
_____
_____

Tuesday

_____
_____
_____

Wednesday

_____
_____
_____

Thursday

_____
_____
_____

Friday

_____
_____
_____

POETRY FROM THE HEART OF THE PROPHETESS

Debra A. JORDAN

Perplexities

What can I do, and who am I? For if I seek to live my life I will destroy it, and if I seek to save myself, I, in turn, become the loser. Woe is me, for I am undone, and troubles abound all around. I will to sink and lose my mind. For all my rage is nothing more that my fears being unmasked; I am discovering the real truth of my feeling of limited humanness. Yet my Divinity speaks from within the city of my soul and declares, "Peace. Be still. Stand in the midst of adversity." For it's in the perplexities of things that I find myself, understanding the greatness of my God. Yes, the mirror has been marred and cracked, but I will not walk with my head hung down. I rise above calamity. I will breathe and blow the winds of peace to clear away the debris of disappointment and disillusionment. Today, my mind and thoughts are clear, so I say again to my soul, "Peace. Be Still." This life that I now lead is my training ground for perfection.

Prophetic Reflections

Weekly Journal

Monday

Tuesday

Wednesday

Thursday

Friday

POETRY FROM THE HEART OF THE PROPHETESS

Debra A. JORDAN

Why Are You Committing Crimes Against Yourself?

Why Are You Allowing Life to Pass You By?

I do not want you to keep letting life pass you by. Jesus said, "I come that ye might have life and have it more abundantly." I am always in search of the things that will quench my thirst, and my hunger for truth. A perpetual question asks about this and asks about that. What is beauty, but ugliness turned inside out? Is what I see real or is it false? Have I become one with the illusion of my truth? Oh, how the mighty have fallen, because of the pride of falsehood. How do I stand and survive the obstacles of my dilemmas?

I won't complain, nor will I walk and be ashamed, for there are no tears to shed. It's just a play on words. Beauty is in the eyes of the beholder, so since I am the beholder, I perceive my vision to be the truth. There is nothing that appears to be real; for what I see is just the illusions of myself superimposed upon realities.

Stop! Hold on! Wait just one minute, for if I close my eyes to what is not, I reacquaint myself to Spirit. And if I listen ever so attentively, I can hear Spirit whispering the essence of truth in my ears. I know of a certainty that what I am looking for lies deep inside of me. I am not on a quest for materiality, but my search seeks the embodiment of truth and Spirit. The answer to my quest lies within my own soul. All my answers are waiting to stand and proclaim what the Holy Spirit has decreed, for only His Word can ever be my reality.

Debra A. JORDAN

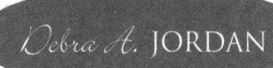

Weekly Journal

Monday

_____
_____
_____

Tuesday

_____
_____
_____

Wednesday

_____
_____
_____

Thursday

_____
_____
_____

Friday

_____
_____
_____

Why Are You Committing Crimes...?

Prophetic Reflections

Weekly Journal

Monday

Tuesday

Wednesday

Thursday

Friday

POETRY FROM THE HEART OF THE PROPHETESS

Debra A. JORDAN

The Drums of Exaltation

Beating the drums of my determination beats a rhythm that stimulates my soul's delight. For in the shout, the drum beat steadily. It never wavers nor skips; I rejoice in its steadiness. Don't stop beating, for you are tapping my jubilation of understanding. I am dancing with myself for myself; touching all so that I might heal them, for I cannot heal that which I have not felt or known. I dance in celebration of my life's journey. The drums are beating and causing me to dance in the totality of my being-ness; I have taken flight in the direction of happiness, peace, and joy. As the drums pulsate, I yield and allow the sound to penetrate and procreate as I dance to the new song of my soul. No one is standing in my way, for each step I take is a step into my future. Every leap I take reveals the glory of my destiny. I and the drum have become one; we celebrate the merging of the beat that infuses me with purpose. It is a ceremony of Divine Intervention.

Debra A. JORDAN

Marriage

Marriage is the one-self talking to it-self. Marriage is only for those that are mature; it is not for babes, nor for the selfish, for you must be skilled in grace. It is the consummation of two selves to become one soul, forever united. It is the mending of the heart, soul, and mind. It is the ultimate act of service and sacrifice. Therefore, you must enter this sacred order with pure reverence. You must understand the Oneness of the union as an unselfish act of love. It's the undressing of the selves to the nudity of motives in order to be redressed in holiness and truth. It's the evolution of death and life unfolding into unity.

Marriage is the elixir of the abundant life. For herein does the mystery unfold; God hides Himself in your sacred journey of togetherness. Marriage causes one to bind oneself only to experience the inexplicable ecstasy of the blissfulness of liberation being "naked and not ashamed." We learn to see ourselves as our Heavenly Father sees us in the completed state of perpetual happiness. Marriage is the reward of obedience, for it bestows the promotion that permits you to rule and reign in the heavens.

Prophetic Reflections

Weekly Journal

Monday

Tuesday

Wednesday

Thursday

Friday

POETRY FROM THE HEART OF THE PROPHETESS

Debra A. JORDAN

The All-ness

It's in the all-ness that you find God. You cannot go halfway or part of the way. It is all or nothing at all; for He has decreed by His Own Self that "He is a jealous God" and "Beside Him there is none other." So I say to Spirit, "Take all of me; allow me to lose myself in and through You. Permit me to submerge myself in Your glorious works. Allow me to drink in Your splendor, so I will never want for anything or anyone. How marvelous are You, my Lord and my King, for I shall boldly declare the truth of You to all who pass by! I count myself worthy to be called by Thy Name."

Prophetic Reflections

Weekly Journal

Monday

_____
_____
_____

Tuesday

_____
_____
_____

Wednesday

_____
_____
_____

Thursday

_____
_____
_____

Friday

_____
_____
_____

POETRY FROM THE HEART OF THE PROPHETESS

Debra A. JORDAN

Sister Wisdom

Wisdom is my company; she is my constant companion in all I do. She allows me to lay my head on her breast so that I may apply myself to understanding. She teaches me by precept and example, for there is nothing hidden from her eyes. She sees all and knows all. She stands strong in all her beauty. She has dressed me in royalty and in completeness. I am filled unto overflowing with new insights from heaven. There is never a need or want in my life, for she's the Master Inventor of creation. She shouts to my soul, "Victory and breakthrough!"

"My sister, my friend, I embrace you... for you are my completing strength...I love you. There's none to compare to you, for I call you my many faces of greatness. You propel me into my purpose and destiny. Let us converse and make merry in our hearts. Every fiber and cell in my being rejoices in your constant companionship.

Prophetic Reflections

There's no room for error or disaster, for everything follows in its rightful course. You are the guiding force of my own handiwork. Even before I was conceived in my mother's womb, you cuddled me with life and encircled me with your breath of strength. It was with great intensity and vigor that you beckoned me from out of the darkness that I found most satisfying. You did call me by my sacred name that no one else knew but me, and in the call I was compelled to answer. I knew by the Spirit that I was prepared and ready to come forth for such a time as this. Wisdom has already said that it was the right time to appear. My sister has called and presented me upon the stage of life. She gives me a standing ovation....

Debra A. JORDAN

Weekly Journal

Monday

Tuesday

Wednesday

Thursday

Friday

Sister Wisdom

Debra A. JORDAN

Rejection

I have feelings of sadness ...I am lost and dejected. I'm in a hole of darkness and there is no one there but my stillness. My voice isn't heard nor is spoken. I have been pushed aside and left to myself. I am heavy in spirit, soul, and body, for I lie in my own pool of regret. For my countenance does betray my inner turmoil; my confidence has been shattered completely. My voice has become unfamiliar to my familiars. I ask myself, "Is there a bondsman to redeem me and take away my pain?"

I cry and weep....Where is my salvation and strength? I am weak from bending and tender from reaching. I walk in disillusionment, for I am weary of the mayhem. I call out loud and clear, but who will stop and hear my supplications? I will not rush to embrace an easy comfort, for where can I go to find peace? Where can I go to escape the hurt that I feel and where can I go to escape the throbbing pain of in my soul? I crave for the peace of release. Dear Lord, You are my balm of Gilead, and my Surety.

Prophetic Reflections

Weekly Journal

Monday

Tuesday

Wednesday

Thursday

Friday

POETRY FROM THE HEART OF THE PROPHETESS

Debra A. JORDAN

A Prayer

Thank You, God, for opening my eyes, so that I can speak of Your beauty and judge uprightly; for it was in my delusion that I found You.

Thank You for re-membering me and for putting me back together.

Thank You for giving me a voice when I had no voice.

You gave me hope and peace for my rage and despair. I take delight in knowing Your devouring love for me.

Thank You, God, that my crooked path is made straight and it's no longer convoluted. I know that my journey has already been declared, and You proclaimed it in me.

Thank You for always astounding my mind, and causing it to be elevated into new heights of understanding. For when I think I have it all, and think I know it all, You just turn and smile at me, and You show me a new

Prophetic Reflections

side of the infinite secrets of Your glory. I embrace Your mysteries wholeheartedly, for knowing and loving You is what I do best.

Thank You, for my worst days are over and there's only blessing and miracles upon my horizon.

Thank You…

Debra A. JORDAN

Weekly Journal

Monday

_____
_____
_____

Tuesday

_____
_____
_____

Wednesday

_____
_____
_____

Thursday

_____
_____
_____

Friday

_____
_____
_____

A Prayer

Prophetic Reflections

POETRY FROM THE HEART OF THE PROPHETESS

… Debra A. JORDAN

Essence

I look into the mirror of eternity as it displays the past, present, and future. I behold the splendor of life unfolding and reproducing itself over and over. One cannot destroy it; nor can you speak evil or ill of it. Just accept it, for the love of life is here to promote you. By acceptance, I have learned to live my life and not merely exist in a world filled with illusions and falsehoods. I know that nothing is impossible, but that all is possible as long as I walk in the light of God's understanding. Nothing is ever hidden nor is it ever lost, for there is a never-ending cycle of metamorphosis in life. I am bubbling over, for I am full of life, and life is full of me. Every morning I behold the newness of opportunity. I am beholding The Greatest Show On Earth in the creation of all things. Creation swallows up the void of nothingness and emptiness. I stand in awe of the totality of continual acts of God's formation. I am listening for Truth, and I implore Thee, "Speak to me, and make it plain."

Prophetic Reflections

Weekly Journal

Monday

Tuesday

Wednesday

Thursday

Friday

POETRY FROM THE HEART OF THE PROPHETESS

Innocence

Innocence has clothed itself in the formless. Innocence is darkness without form and implodes without structure.

There was a time when I, the innocent, did drink and lap up your words. I knew within myself as I testified of your greatness that there was none to compare to the greatness of you. For you stood tall and grand in all your doings. Your words were sweeter than honey. Your peace became my peace, for you clothed me for the purpose wherein I was called. All of creation did rejoice and sing forth the praises of our King, for Innocence met Greatness, and the two became one.....

Prophetic Reflections

Weekly Journal

Monday

_____
_____
_____

Tuesday

_____
_____
_____

Wednesday

_____
_____
_____

Thursday

_____
_____
_____

Friday

_____
_____
_____

POETRY FROM THE HEART OF THE PROPHETESS

Debra A. JORDAN

Frustration

Damn the steps that take you nowhere but yet cause you to sweetly digress from intention.

Damn the talking that produces no results by damning the ways that we have walked in.

Damn you, damn the now and what was and what might have been.

I'm damning everything that should have and could have been, for this is abomination.

Yesterday was and is no more, for it has faded into oblivion.

Damn the angry men and angry woman and the angry children who sit by the wayside and do nothing but wallow in the excrement of their rage....

Damn the mother who is distressing about her wayward child...

Prophetic Reflections

Damn the boss that is trying to meet a deadline....

Forget about the past, present, and future. Allow that which you forget to redeem those past failures. There is a resurrection of all things, but it must first start with the inner you taking the first step...for all is vanity…

Debra A. JORDAN

Weekly Journal

Monday

Tuesday

Wednesday

Thursday

Friday

Frustration

Debra A. JORDAN

Age

Age is just a pair of numbers or symbols having fun with themselves. It is just a game they like to play....don't you see? Do you not understand? There is 1, there's 2, and the rest of the gang are dwelling in their matrix being everywhere and yet nowhere in the playpen of time. They are always hoping that you get to the point. What is that point? Who knows or who cares? But I have found the secret and heard the whispers; they all are trying to get back to the point of zero. For within that mysterious number zero dwells an endless cycle. And with the zero of infinity there are endless cycles and possibilities. Numbers are all the same— trying to embrace their identity which is only found within endless possibilities.

Don't you know that we are all ageless; we are not bound to a digit. But we must embrace the numbers of age in order to be complete. So we came to earth to experience age, for after everything has been said or done, we will return to the great mystery of our beloved spirit and watch the numbers continue their game....

Prophetic Reflections

Weekly Journal

Monday

_____
_____
_____

Tuesday

_____
_____
_____

Wednesday

_____
_____
_____

Thursday

_____
_____
_____

Friday

_____
_____
_____

POETRY FROM THE HEART OF THE PROPHETESS

Debra A. JORDAN

Who?

I am in a state of pondering the "Who" of things. You are a mind and yet you belong to no one. Not even me, for "Who" is the question and "Who" is the answer within itself. It's strange, but yet familiar in its own peculiar and wondrous way. "Who" goes deeper than what others may say or do. The flower blooms and shows forth its beauty. The uniqueness is that the flower and nature ask no questions; they just do that which they have been created to do. Nature never asks or questions; it just is and wants to be.

What has been decreed? It's Who that starts the question; not understanding it was created to bring confirmation of what is and has been. For the Who must say yes to the universe, and not be swayed by any other. The Who gives you the option to look outside of your self — never to bring the peace or the I am-ness to the question of oneness. You cannot be one as long as concerns are ruminating in your mind. You must dwell in the being-ness of your innermost self. There you will

Prophetic Reflections

encounter peace like a river and the stillness of the flow. Where am I? I cannot tell, for time is no more as long as Who has found my place of satisfaction. Step into the timeless ageless of the now. Spirit beckons you, and you must obey. The Who's Who does not need to be left alone because it is tired of being the beginning of the start of the word. Who must find its place in the scheme of things....understanding is the beginning of wisdom. Understand the Who, and never look into other places to search for the truth of being.

Debra A. JORDAN

Weekly Journal

Monday

Tuesday

Wednesday

Thursday

Friday

Who?

130

Debra A. JORDAN

Love Walk

Let me not count the ways, for I love thee more than life itself. My imagination is full of My Savior's love. You are the Light that illuminates my path. You give me hope when my way seems dim and dark. And when I think that it's enough, You speak a Word and give me a thought that tells me to stay and wait just a little longer. For even in my dreams, You are there. You are ever-present, whispering sweetness to my soul. For Your touch possesses me day and night. You keep me in a state of ultimate bliss through every day and every night. When I hear other voices, I only hear the One Voice, which is You. You are my Good and Faithful Shepherd. I say and have said I will forever shout it on the mountain top; "YOU ARE MY ALL IN ALL."

Prophetic Reflections

Weekly Journal

Monday

Tuesday

Wednesday

Thursday

Friday

POETRY FROM THE HEART OF THE PROPHETESS

Debra A. JORDAN

My Confession

Yes that's right, I created it all. What have I done and why have I committed such devastations to myself and to my creations? I created the house, the body, the clothes and even the car I drive. I even created my rebellious worrisome children. They are my beautiful evolving formations. Yes they even look and strangely enough act just like me. I'm not afraid to face my fears. I am the master of all my design. I confess that I have lived a life that was beneath me. I was in a stupor, wanting others to do my bidding. I am repenting now and, never to create such illusion for myself. I repent for the living in the lie and thinking that I could not and would not obtain. I repent failing to see the greatness of my God, and judging him as man and not the alpha and the omega, him being God the omnipotent, omnipresence and omniscient one. I confess to the wrongness of my being ness. I must reinstate my divine self hood, in order to right the wrong that I have participated in. I am not blind for I see clearer than I have ever seen

Prophetic Reflections

before. I am the individual, the one at fault in this situation; no one can help me but only me.

The quest is can I behold it and love it enough to deliver to from its unrighteousness. What have been done I can redeem it in a moment of a twinkle of an eye. I must stand in the counsel of the mighty One and change my course of action. I have already dismissed the case of duality that brought me low. I must realign and readjust myself to the point of focusing my energy and my mind on the right things. For only when I change will change transform me? Life is waiting for me to alter my perception of what is and the why of life. Creation is calling me by my divine name to make it whole and complete once again. The conclusion and the certainty of my confession is will I be, and if so when? Selah

Debra A. JORDAN

Weekly Journal

Monday

Tuesday

Wednesday

Thursday

Friday

My Confession

Debra A. JORDAN

Illuminations

The light has come I cannot remain in the shadows any longer. Nor can I remain in my comfort zone. There isn't time for rest and relax for the light beckons me to move forward. The light shines brighter than I can see, wooing me into its heated embrace. Yes the light has over shadowed me making me more alive than I have ever been before. I am enthralled by its beauty and peace. For nothing else can compare to it. I beheld the splendor of it and it would not allow me to look away. I have known that you are the light upon my path, always showing me my directions. The light of my understanding is causing true expressions. This light I see is the captain of my soul. It is wisdom speaking to wisdom, the voiceless voice of reason. I say let it shine in me through and through and convert me into the being I was meant to be. The light does wash me and make me whole again. I bathe myself into the shimmering glory of reality, for this reality I bathe myself in its not earthly nor is it sensual, it's from above. I need no one or anything to

Prophetic Reflections

tell me I am this or I am that, for I walk in my own statehood of knowing. I am beautiful and fearfully fashioned in all of God's glory.

Debra A. JORDAN

Weekly Journal

Monday

Tuesday

Wednesday

Thursday

Friday

Illuminations

Debra A. JORDAN

The Viewer

The question comes to the mind. Am I the participator or the observer of life and its many causes and effects? For with every act there is always the benefit whether good or bad. I know that God is not mocked for whatsoever a mind sows that shall he also reap, it makes no difference it's just the way things are. Am I just a mindless being, just waiting for life to pass me by? Am I my own person? If so why do I continue to listen to those who have no answers or solutions for my many dilemmas? I will never wait to be, or to be held by the trails and dictates of life. So I must remove myself from the deception and pressures of life and return to my first estate. For where I am in this moment of time is only but a false impression. In me lie the infinite promises of God's grace for me and for my household. What do I say to myself, am I the formless one seeking form and expressions? Do I choose to just look and allow the world to pass me by, or do I awake from my slumber and start doing and being. The choice is always left up to me

Prophetic Reflections

and me alone. Do I just put the limitations on myself just to give me the excuse of the why of every day?

No one can stop me for I choose to live my life in remembrance of who I am. I am putting all the pieces of the puzzle of my life back together again perfectly, and in order.

For there is never a right time to do anything, it's just in the moment of true realization.

Debra A. JORDAN

Weekly Journal

Monday

___

Tuesday

___

Wednesday

___

Thursday

___

Friday

___

The Viewer

Debra A. JORDAN

Who Do Men Say I am?

It's my time to identify and to affirm me. I will not permit anything to stand in my way and to speak lies in my ear. They will not declare me, and cause me to become angry and sin. I own no one anything but love. That I will give, for it's the nature of my Father. Some say I am just a woman and wife, others say I am just a mother, sister friend and foe. I say that this is all true but yet there is more. I am in a constant state of unfolding. There is a holy metamorphose that has taken hold of me, and I dare not stop this process. There are some that even said that I was nothing, just a piece of trash. Yes it hurt and yes I did cry, but I heard a voice from on high that told me that it was just someone else's truth. It doesn't matter to me what they say or think about me, it only matters that I know who I am. No one can define me but me, for I am my own person. They all have their own opinions and ideas about me

Prophetic Reflections

but it's their own selves trying to be me; and yet never becoming me. I pronounce that all of men's sayings are just empty proverbs, which are trying to clothe themselves. So I must become deaf to these utterances and move forward because destiny and purpose beckon me; for men babble about everything that is conceivable and yet cannot believe in their own divinity. They speak and pray to dumb idols that have no life of their own. I will not sit quietly and accept these falsehoods about me; I will arise and move onward. I will ascend and take my flight above these saying; for I am the master creator of my own purpose.

Debra A. JORDAN

Weekly Journal

Monday

Tuesday

Wednesday

Thursday

Friday

Who Do Men Say I Am?

148

Debra A. JORDAN

Unstoppable and Invincible

I am the author of my own fate; you can't stop me even if you tried. Why should I die when I can live in the abundance flow of God? I don't have to pass on; I can live and be happy. I don't have to walk in despair but I can have sweet peace. Who said that it would be easy? I don't fight with my hands and weapons of mass destruction; I fight with my mind, for it carries all things I need. I am a most formidable opponent; for it's the sword of faith that I wield skillfully. You know I always like a good challenge. You cannot stop me from fulfilling my purpose. I am invincible. Oh you may slow me down but I will always get back up. You have heard the saying that you can't keep a good woman down, well that's me getting up every time for I must keep myself in check. For after I have done all, I still stand I will never throw in the towel of defeat. I am a winner, for there is no failure in God. The failure always lies in the inability of not seeing God in all things.

Prophetic Reflections

Weekly Journal

Monday

_____
_____
_____

Tuesday

_____
_____
_____

Wednesday

_____
_____
_____

Thursday

_____
_____
_____

Friday

_____
_____
_____

POETRY FROM THE HEART OF THE PROPHETESS

Debra A. Jordan

Me

I am a friend to the friendless, and I am a mother to the motherless. I see what others refuse to see; and my ear only hears wisdom. My arms are open, and I will freely embrace all those in need. Don't look away from me, for in me is life and peace. I will answer all your questions and bring peace and understanding to your soul. You can rest in me for I will give you liberty and freedom. Think it not a strange thing; I am the one that stands in the mist of creation. For I am the hearer and the speaker, I am the healer and the punisher; I am unknown and yet I live in the certainties of the known. I mean no one any harm I am just speaking my mind out loud. No one can harden their heart to my declarations, for my words (are weavers are truths.) My words have no beginning nor ending. My words are alive waiting to be clothed; I am the only one that can give them their attire. I speak and it is so, for I am the representation of life. I stand in the mist of the congregation of the elders and make my own inquires. For I judge the hearts of those that have forgotten me, even

Prophetic Reflections

those who think that they have known me and are worthy of me. I will wait a little while longer so you can take in all that has been said. For I must move on I cannot stand still and wait for you to volunteer, you just have to believe in your potential that has been latent.

Do you not understand my dark sayings, for this is you when you take your place in me?

Debra A. JORDAN

Weekly Journal

Monday

Tuesday

Wednesday

Thursday

Friday

Me

154

Debra A. JORDAN

Talking Rivers

Talking rivers that will not cease; flowing everywhere. And yet desiring and wanting to be heard by all who will listen. You cannot truly stand still and not be affected by the voices of the river. For you and you alone understand that there is a flow to the happenings of life. It doesn't matter whether the talking rivers are raging or whether they are contemplating.

Talking rivers speak to me hold not your sacred decrees from me. Bring understanding to me so I may learn of your fathomless wisdom. For the earth does stand still never giving up her secrets of life. I come to you rivers so you may impart your life to me. Talking rivers command me to stand in the mist of what is not so that I will never be removed from the holiness of my Savior; for I am acquainted with the winds of change. For the wind of change is my unwavering companion. I am not moved by the swaying of the unfamiliar only the flow of life that saturates my being.

Prophetic Reflections

The rivers of life have caused me to set a watch upon my mouth and I will not be afraid not will I speak, only when spirit tells me to; for I stand still and nothing will stop my flow. I stand because this is what I have been called to do, and not anything else matters. I will make my claim to what is rightfully mind. Talking rivers you are the life of my sustenance, and nothing else can substance me. I will cease to speak so that I may hear only the one voice of Peace.

Debra A. JORDAN

Weekly Journal

Monday

Tuesday

Wednesday

Thursday

Friday

Talking Rivers

Debra A. JORDAN

My Soul

Soul, soul speaks to me, for I command my soul to speak her mind and rejoice for she shall make her boast in her God; for the Lord have done great things to me and for me. I will proclaim the wondrous works of my God. My soul does cry out to my God, for no one can quench my thirst and complete me every which way. For my soul does cry the cry of transformation, into the oneness of divinity. For I am a living being fixed on purpose. There is a cry from the bottomless depths of my soul and God has heard me and brought me up and out of my despair. For my soul does mirror the reflection of the many possibilities of spirit. It is the inner reflections of spirit breaking through the illusions of time and space. My soul is in states of contemplation of becoming, the whole.

For I have found my delight in him. Let us dance the dance of life and be glad, for there's no death but the enfoldment of creation. Don't tell me to be quiet for

Prophetic Reflections

it's my soul that makes her boast in her God. It's my soul that must speak her peace. It's my soul that must take flight into the heavens. It's my soul that does ponder the infinite greatness of her maker. For my soul will continue to speak her truth forever more blesses.

Debra A. JORDAN

Weekly Journal

Monday

Tuesday

Wednesday

Thursday

Friday

My Soul